MA

Building the Fistic Edge
in Competition & Self-Defense
for Men & Women

Mark Hatmaker

Cover and interior photos by Doug Werner

Tracks Publishing
San Diego, California

Boxing for MMA
Building the Fistic Edge in Competition
& Self-Defense for Men & Women
Mark Hatmaker

Tracks Publishing
140 Brightwood Avenue
Chula Vista, CA 91910
619-476-7125
tracks@cox.net
www.startupsports.com
trackspublishing.com

Copyright © 2014 by Mark Hatmaker and Doug Werner
10 9 8 7 6 5 4 3 2 1

Publisher's Cataloging-in-Publication

Hatmaker, Mark.

Boxing for MMA : building the fistic edge in competition & self-defense for men & women / Mark Hatmaker ; cover and interior photos by Doug Werner. -- San Diego, California : Tracks Publishing, [2014]

pages ; cm.

ISBN: 978-1-935937-62-3
Includes index.
Summary: This manual serves a dual purpose. First, it is a boxing primer to review (or discover) the boxing basics including stance, footwork, punches and combinations; and the flip side: defenses and counters for each fistic attack. Second, it takes these boxing skills and shoots them through an MMA prism that addresses the realities of mixed martial arts competition or combat. This guide will be your go-to resource for absorbing the boxing game and blending those skills into your MMA fighting arsenal.Publisher.

1. Mixed martial arts--Training. 2. Hand-to-hand fighting--Training. 3. Boxing--Training. 4. Boxers (Sports)--Training. 5. Martial arts--Training. 6. Self-defense--Training. I. Werner, Doug, 1950- II. Title. III. Title: Boxing for mixed martial arts.

GV1102.7.M59 H384 2014   2014950787
796.815--dc23   1411

Books by Mark Hatmaker

No Holds Barred Fighting:
The Ultimate Guide to Submission Wrestling

More No Holds Barred Fighting:
Killer Submissions

No Holds Barred Fighting:
Savage Strikes

No Holds Barred Fighting:
Takedowns

No Holds Barred Fighting:
The Clinch

No Holds Barred Fighting:
The Ultimate Guide to Conditioning

No Holds Barred Fighting:
The Kicking Bible

No Holds Barred Fighting:
The Book of Essential Submissions

Boxing Mastery

No Second Chance:
A Reality-Based Guide to Self-Defense

MMA Mastery:
Flow Chain Drilling and Integrated O/D Training

MMA Mastery:
Ground and Pound

MMA Mastery:
Strike Combinations

Boxer's Book of Conditioning & Drilling

Boxer's Bible of Counterpunching

Mud, Guts & Glory
Tips & Training for Extreme Obstacle Racing

She's Tough
Extreme Fitness Training for Women

*Books are available through major bookstores
and booksellers on the Internet.*

To the late Shawn Tompkins, one helluva of an MMA striking coach. He was about as streamlined and forward thinking as they come. Condolences to his family, friends and crew.

Acknowledgments
Phyllis Carter
Editor Extraordinaire

Kylie Hatmaker
Partner in all things

Contents

How to use the MMA Mastery manuals

This book and the others in this series are meant to be used in an interlocking, synergistic manner where the sum value of the manuals is greater than the individual parts. What we are striving to do with each manual is to focus on a specific aspect of the twin sports of MMA/submission wrestling and give thoughtful consideration to the necessary ideas, tactics and strategies pertinent to the facet of focus. We are aware that this piecemeal approach may seem lacking if one only consumes one or two manuals at most, but we are confident that once three or more manuals have been studied, the overall picture or method will begin to reveal itself.

Since the manuals are interlocking there is no single manual in the series that is meant to be complete in and of itself. For example, although *No Holds Barred Fighting: Savage Strikes* is a thorough compendium on NHB/self-defense striking, it is bolstered with side-by-side study of *Boxing Mastery*. While the book *More No Holds Barred Fighting: Killer Submissions* introduces the idea of chaining submissions and can be used as a solitary tool, it is made all the stronger by an understanding of the material that preceded it in the first submission manual. I will say that two later books in this series, *Boxer's Book of Conditioning & Drilling* and *Boxer's Bible of Counterpunching* are especially meant to lock in with *MMA for Boxing*.

OK. Enough with the methodology. Let's lace up the gloves!

Boxing for MMA

> ... separation of training, while allowing an athlete to hone a particular facet of the game, ignores the first "M" in MMA, which ... stands for mixed.

Intro: Boxing for MMA

I think you can guess from the title of this manual what we'll be focused on this time, but I still want to clarify a few things. First of all, this manual is all about Boxing *for* MMA and not Boxing *in addition to* MMA. What do I mean by that?

Often the distinct and disparate elements of MMA are instructed and/or trained as if they were separate sports in a cross-training fashion that the fighter/athlete is expected to meld spontaneously in the face of fire. For example, a typical MMA class schedule may show a session for Jiu-Jitsu and wrestling, another session for clinch work and boxing and another separate session for Muay Thai and free rolling.

Yes, the preceding broad categories of combat sports are all important elements of MMA, but this separation of training, while allowing an athlete to hone a particular facet of the game, ignores the first "M" in MMA,

Here we strive to take one (and only one) important aspect of the game and address how to train it to blend, to mix seamlessly with the rest of your MMA game.

which as we all know stands for mixed. Just where exactly is the mix in this sort of separation represented by the above schedule?

There is wisdom in emphasizing certain targets of focus within any sport, but making them too far removed from other aspects of the game may not allow the burgeoning athlete/fighter to meld them as speedily or intelligently as we hope for. At the very least we should blend as many different aspects as we can manage into a single session so that we hone to the specificity principle of conditioning/training, which dictates that the more closely we adhere to what the sport/game conditions actually are, the greater success we will have in manifesting our hard-worked skills under pressure. There is a Special Forces Maxim that states this beautifully:

"Let your training be reflective of battlefield conditions."

I have witnessed good athletes who are subjected to

"separate but equal" training schedules box well on boxing night and shoot well on takedown night and roll well on roll night, but when it came to MMA scrimmage night, well, you could sometimes see the visible shift between sports with little stutters and shudders as if the fighter's combat transmission needed a visit to the mechanic.

Now this transmission slipping problem will in all likelihood disappear as more time and experience are garnered, but would we not be doing the fighter a greater service by taking good care of that transmission from the get-go? This sort of transmission preventative maintenance is exactly what we have in mind with this manual. Here we strive to take one (and only one) important aspect of the game and address how to train it to blend, to mix seamlessly with the rest of your MMA game.

No balky transmissions for this crew.

Separate will not equal equal

Let's flog a dead horse. The late legendary Brazilian Jiu-Jitsu coach Carlson Gracie offered the following wisdom:

"Punch a Jiu-Jitsu black belt in the face once and he becomes a brown belt, punch him twice and he becomes a purple belt."

Mr. Gracie is calling our attention to the fact that even a combat sport as formidable as BJJ can leave a skilled competitor coming up short in the face of the combat mix. And, of course, this entropy of single sports/art under fire does not hold only for BJJ.

The boxer who has never faced a takedown in his life is going down.

The wrestler who has never taken a full-on educated hook to the chin is going down.

The BJJ black belt who has never tasted the femur-bruising thud of a trained Muay Thai leg kick is going down.

The Sambo practitioner who has never tasted a solid uppercut to the liver is going down.

All effective arts/sports are subject to entropy if the competitor has never had experience with the newly introduced mix.

To combat Mr. Gracie's observation, we see fighters and trainers wisely training outside of their root game, but often this is what leads to the cross-training problem we previously mentioned. There seems to be an assumption for some that training good pure BJJ and training good pure Muay Thai will create a double threat. Maybe, maybe not. Again, what is missing is the mix.

Let's go back to Mr. Gracie's wisdom. The BJJ black belt does not simply need the overlay of a good striking game to stop the devaluing of his black belt to a brown belt. He needs a striking game that dovetails and accents his current striking game — one that has modifications made in the striking for his Jiu-Jitsu and one

> It is the mix itself that informs the intelligent fighters and trainers of the world just what is worth keeping in each art [and] what needs to be thrown on the scrap heap ...

that has modifications in his grappling for the striking.

Pure BJJ will not work for this mixed martial artist, and pure striking (whether boxing or Muay Thai) will not do the job either. All combat arts/sports have their weaknesses revealed when the mix is introduced. It is the mix itself that informs the intelligent fighters and trainers of the world just what is worth keeping in each art, what needs to be thrown on the scrap heap and what needs to be modified.

A case for boxing only

All right, since I am making a case for a mix being superior to single disciplines, why the obsessive focus on boxing — a punching game to be your go-to in striking?

Logically and pragmatically shouldn't we look for Muay Thai or kickboxing as the inclusion of knees and kicks would seem to provide more mix than boxing?

Sure, an argument can easily and perhaps not unwisely be made to go that route.

But allow me to plead my idiosyncratic case.

First — I am not making a case for pure boxing. What we are presenting in these pages is Boxing Plus. That is, the standard boxing arsenal *plus* elbows, hammer-fists and a few other unorthodox blows. This gets us a bit closer to the mix.

The hands are where the KOs are.

Second — Boxing has an "easier" (easy being relative) skill set to learn and master than complete integration of kicking and good boxing. We are striving to make you as formidable a striker as we can manage in the quickest time possible. Hence, our Boxing Plus streamline.

Third — The Boxing Plus approach is also faster in the actual speed sense of the word. Firing punches requires less set up from the body than kicking and we can launch single shots and rapid-fire combinations more quickly. Think punches in bunches — the more shots fired increases the chances of damage. Saving up for big shots (the big punch or the big kick) might be too much of all your eggs in one basket thinking.

Fourth — Boxing Plus is more mobile, and mobility often leads to a stronger offense and defense. Kicks must be set from the feet and hips and more footwork adjustments must be accounted for to make this a primary aspect of your game. Kicking footwork sets up kicking and little else. Boxing Plus footwork can set up your striking and takedown capabilities. Let alone the fact that no matter how speedy your kicks are, the mere act of throwing a kick makes you a one-legged fighter.

Fifth — As we mentioned above, the Boxing Plus stance and footwork allows you to transition seamlessly between striking and takedowns. It also allows you the ability to transition from striking to takedown defense easily. This ease of shifting between boxing and grappling may be just the reason why we see so many elite wrestlers overlay a boxing game onto their superior grappling skills.

Sixth — The hands are where the KOs are. In a prior book, *No Holds Barred Fighting: The Book of Essential Submissions*, we surveyed 640 elite level fights to quantify just what exactly did and did not work. Overwhelmingly strikes via the hands, whether on the feet or on the ground, won top honors by a long shot. If you want the statistical breakdown that informs this fact, have a look at that book. If you want to take my word for it, striking via the hands out-performs kicking, knees, elbows and submissions. No, I'm not saying that we need none of these other facets. I'm stating the empirical fact that throwing the hands wins lots and lots of fights, so let's make sure we are as good with this skill as we can be.

Seventh — UFC 168, Chris Weidman vs. Anderson Silva 2. Need I say more? This was the leg-kick-gone-wrong injury heard round the world. Yes, such injuries are a rarity, but as more and more athletes are adopting a destruction mode of checking the leg kick (as opposed to simply block checking), this is definitely food for thought. We will be educating such destructive leg checks in this manual. (We won't kick, but we do want to be prepared for the kick).

BTW — It's not only Silva's injury that should inform our bias for the hands, Jose Maria's right knee in his bout with John Lineker is another lesson in the possible perils of leg kicking.

To be fair, boxers have broken their hands in fights, but more often than not the fighter is able to finish despite such injuries whereas some of the more devastating leg injuries are bout enders.

And to be fair yet again, we do have the most unusual and one-of-a-kind self-induced injury via boxing, the shoulder dislocation of Chan Sung Jung when he fought Jose Aldo in a featherweight championship bout (UFC 163).

Yes, statistically the self-injury via strikes (boxing or kicking) is low, but I predict that we will see more and more fighters adopt Weidman's hard-to-ignore use of modified destructive checking to provide a disincentive for kicking.

1. *"You've got to walk before you can run,* **but you've got to stand before you can walk"**

Any discussion of stance worth its salt has to use Good Athletic Position (GAP) as the default starting base. For the uninitiated, GAP is the fundamentally sound mechanical position that the body assumes when it is expected to perform optimally across a variety of stressors. These stressors can be a sudden vertical jump, a quick explosive lift, a preparation to move to either direction laterally, a transition to back-pedaling, et cetera. The key to GAP is that it is a preparation for variety — a start point for options if you will.

> Stance is an athletic start point ...

Task Specific Positions (TSP) begin with the end in mind. That is, the sprinter knows which direction the body must move, the batter knows the approximate plane he must swing into, the fighter setting up the spin kick knows where and how she must set the hips to facilitate the smooth pirouette. Still, even with TSP there are, usually, only minor adjustments from GAP, and this close adherence is for good reason.

GAP wisely adheres to an equal distribution of weight so that movement in any cardinal direction can be smoothly transitioned into. Too much weight over any given foot slows the transition into that direction.

... that travels with you wherever you go. Stance is every step you take. Stance is every punch you throw.

GAP's equal distribution of weight not only optimizes mobility, it increases access to power. Full body commitment is already realized by having both feet underneath the hips. GAP allows for quick power access to any given side by this same equal distribution of weight. If I am running a 70/30 stance (70 percent of weight over the rear foot and 30 percent over the lead) I've got to make up that distribution when I go for lead-side strikes. In my 50/50 GAP position, a flex of the rear calf and a pelvic torque loads me for power.

OK, I've rhapsodized GAP as the way to go with stance, but I want to stretch this idea further. There is a tendency in some combat disciplines to pay a lot of attention to stance as if it were an isolated element. That is, "OK, here is our stance, got it? Looks good. Now, here is some other stuff to learn." I'm pleading a case for not thinking of stance as a stock-still element, but rather an athletic position that informs all of your movement. After all, what good is a stance if it no longer supports your offense or defense as soon as you take your first step? Fights happen on the move. MMA is not some Karate Kid crane stance adolescent fantasy.

With every step you take, with every punch you throw, with every takedown you stuff, with every move you make, in an ideal world, you should be analyzing it for GAP and making adjustments whenever and wherever possible to adhere as closely as you can manage to perfection. Always be asking questions about GAP in your training.

Are you falling into your punches rather than stepping into them? If the answer is falling, I smell an easily countered fighter and/or a weighted lead leg rife for leg-kick punishment.

Is your lateral movement overloaded when you move? A leg kick or a Lyoto Machida-style foot sweep will bring that foolishness to the mat.

Is the lead foot light? Sounds like someone is inviting the takedown.

Is the stance too high? Again, takedown city.

Any deviation from GAP acts either as a situation to be countered or information about your intentions.

Stance, although similar to the word stand, is not really about how you stand.

Stance is an athletic start point that travels with you wherever you go. Stance is every step you take. Stance is every punch you throw.

Modified Boxing Plus stance

The Boxing for MMA or Boxing Plus stance needs to be altered a bit from the standard boxing stance as the MMA competitor has more concerns than the straight boxer. Let's get to it.

● Take one natural step forward with your lead foot (the foot that you prefer to have up front when you fight).
● Feel the weight through the balls of your feet. You won't necessarily raise the heels off the mat, but you don't want to be a flat-footed fighter. Flat feet are slow feet.
● Pivot ever so slightly on the balls of your feet toward your inside — that is toward your chest side. The Boxing Plus stance is a little more forward facing than a standard boxing stance, but we don't want to be so square that we invite unobstructed front kicks.
● Give a slight bend to the knees. This leg coiling will supply us with mobility speed and preload our punches for power.
● Adhere to a 50/50 GAP weight distribution.
● Keep your feet under your hips.
Upper body positioning
● Forearms parallel. A common error (perhaps as common as drifting the hands low) is creating an inverted **V**, where the forearms move apart toward the elbows. This invites shots to the liver.
● Keep your rear hand on your jaw.
● Your lead hand will be held forward of your lead shoulder at the same level as your lead shoulder.
● The lead shoulder is carried a bit high to protect your jaw. Think holding a phone hands-free, pinched between your lead shoulder and chin.
Head Positioning
● Tuck your chin toward your chest. It will not rest directly on it. Simply tuck it toward the chest an inch or two.
● When you have your eyes on your opponent, there should always be a little of your brow or upper orbital socket in your sightline.

Nope

Boxing Plus Stance
All good except for image left.
Inverted **V** of arms invites body
blows.

2. Footwork concepts

We labored footwork to death in *Boxing Mastery.* Here we will educate a stripped down Boxing Plus footwork approach in our focus pad drills, but there are a few broad concepts to keep in mind in all Boxing Plus movement.

Step & drag

Forget bouncing, shuffling, staying up on the toes and shoe-shining with your footwork. Such light, high-base work will work against you in MMA.

Too high in your stance and movement? You're welcoming the takedown.

Too bouncy and light on the toes? Hello, again, to the takedown.

We need you solid, but solid does not mean stiff and immobile. Far from it. To keep you in solid contact with the planet earth, we need to adhere to the step & drag protocol that is essentially ...

● Any direction you want to move, you will step the foot nearest to that direction first.
● This is immediately followed by dragging/sliding the trail foot back into GAP stance position.

To reiterate:
● If you want to advance, move the lead foot first, then drag the rear foot.
● To retreat, the rear foot steps first and then the lead foot is dragged into position.
● To move right, the right foot moves first,
● And to move left, the left foot moves first.

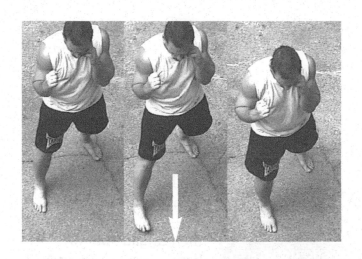

Stepping & dragging up, back, side to side.

OK, the next little bit of footwork advice may be the most important advice in this book — so pay attention. Read it twice, or once a week, whatever it takes to sink this lesson in.

Fundamental locomotion

The best boxers of the "sweet science" variety as opposed to the slugger breed are noted for their nimble footwork to maneuver themselves into firing position and then to glide out of harm's way. As a matter of fact, the "sweet" in "sweet science" refers to "sweet" movement. That is, the apparent ability to dance, glide, shift, bob, weave, duck and pivot out of danger with apparent ease. Referring to a fighter "as sweet as sugar" (as in Sugar Ray Robinson, Sugar Ray Leonard and Sugar Shane Mosely) is not a comment on their table manners. A sweet fighter or a sugary fighter has got smooth, efficient footwork.

> If there is only one bit of footwork/positional wisdom that you pick up from this manual it would be this:
>
> *Circle Away From The Power Side.*

Boxing has approximately 14 distinct footwork maneuvers that the sweetest of fighters have under their belts. The fewer of these steps a boxer knows and utilizes, the less sweet he or she may be. Of these 14 steps, about half of them call for an upright posture

that won't work for MMA. This is good news for the
MMA fighter as that means we have halved the skill set
allowing us to get to mastery in less time.

Don't fall into the trap of thinking more is better and
that if you go ahead and train all 14 you'll have an
advantage. Maybe, maybe not. The approximate half of
the 14 steps we will ignore are movements that
evolved in a sport that never had to worry about the
leg kick or the takedown or a clinch that was used for
anything more than tying up or to rest. We have culled
the herd for good reason.

If there is only one bit of footwork/positional wisdom
that you pick up from this manual it would be this:

Circle Away From The Power Side.

The lightness of MMA gloves has equalized the power
in both hands to some degree (mainly by raising the
power of the lead hand and doing nothing to minimize
the rear hand.) But this equalization of power in no
way overturns the laws of physics. The rear hand and
rear leg have a greater distance to travel. Rear shots
come with more wind up and muscular torque than
lead punches.

With the truth of physics in mind, we should observe
the following rules:

When fighting an opponent who fights with the left
side forward, you would be wise to emphasize moving
to your right.

When fighting an opponent who fights with the right side forward, flip this advice and move to your left. As in grappling, move toward your opponent's back whenever and wherever possible.

A little case study to bring this lesson home.

UFC 166, the bout between Gilbert Melendez and Diego Sanchez.

These two warriors are tough as they come, willing to bang like nobody's business (as they do in this bout.) Go ahead and queue it up if you don't mind. Before you view it, here's what I want you to keep your eyes on. Mr. Sanchez moves away from Mr. Melendez's power side approximately once of his own accord. Once.

As the fight moves into its final round, freeze frame any shot where you have only the right side of Diego's face showing. It'll look good, like he's not even been in a fight. Next, freeze-frame the left side. What does that open maw of a cut tell you? That puffed cheek?

It tells you that either Melendez is slick as can be with that rear hand (and he's no slouch), or that Diego has been walking into the power side all night long. It's the latter.

I find this tragic because Diego is undeniably an excellent fighter with grit to spare, but only once in this bout does he take steps (literally, steps) to minimize the damage being done. What's all the more tragic is that his celebrated corner does not mention the obvious. By

> **... the best boxing trainers know that a good fighter is built from the feet up.**

all means, watch the corner talk and tell me if you hear one bit of advice about this most basic bit of boxing knowledge — walk away from the power.

Melendez wins this fight and rightfully so, but the outcome may have been different if someone in Diego's corner had simply told him to circle right.

Keep your feet under you

This subheading should be about as obvious a piece of advice as you're ever going to hear, but the longer you play this game, the more you'll realize it is not adhered to as often as you would think.

Some of the best boxing trainers know that a good fighter is built from the feet up. As a good rule of thumb, when first evaluating a fighter/opponent, observe the feet when they are working drills (particularly pad drills). No matter how loud the bang is on the pad, if the feet are awry, you've got a fighter that can be exploited.

The Boxing Plus stance is not quite as relaxed as it looks. In an effort to keep your weight distribution as close to perfect GAP as possible, let's approach our stance and movement in the following manner.

- Imagine yourself standing in your sock feet on a freshly waxed floor.
- Pull with your lead foot as if you could slide the ball of the foot toward the heel of the rear foot.
- Pull with your rear foot aiming the ball of the foot toward the toes of the lead foot.

Of course, not being in our socks on a waxed floor there will be no movement. But feel the tension — that's what I want you to feel through every stance iteration and every step you take.

Tension ... step ... drag ... tension.

This may seem like a small tip, but if you follow this scrupulously, particularly in your focus mitt drills, this is a game changer for speed, balance and power.

3. Boxing Plus arsenal

Let's get down to the primary tools in the Boxing Plus arsenal and how to throw them with malicious intent. Make sure you use GAP — feet underneath throughout to optimize performance.

Jab to the head

● Fire the punch straight from the on-guard position turning the fist over so that on contact the palm is facing downward.
● You will rotate the hips and pivot on the balls of the feet toward your inside/chest.
● Return the punch (the negative aspect) along the same path.

All punches are thrown from and retract to the on-guard position shown above.

Cross / rear straight to the head

● Fire the punch from the on-guard position straight toward your target, turning your fist over to face downward on contact.

● Your lead fist retracts to touch your jaw as the cross is extended.

● Pivot on the balls of your feet to turn toward your outside/back.

● The rear heel will raise slightly, but you will not neglect the slide/squeeze between your feet.

● Retract along the same path.

Lead hook to the head

● Raise your lead elbow until it is approximately horizontal with your target.

● You will have a 90-degree angle in the punching arm.

● Pivot toward your inside punching with the arm as a single fused limb. Don't extend the arm.

● The palm can be facing downward or toward you upon impact.

Rear hook to the head

● The same mechanics as the lead hook, but here we pull the lead hand to the jaw as we fire.

Lead uppercut

● Your arm is a 90-degree fused piece of bone like the hooks.
● Dip and lean your lead shoulder toward your target.
● Fire the punch from the knees first, followed by a hip extension and finally the shoulder punching the fused arm along a vertical plane.
● As with the hook, there is no need to extend the arm or exaggerate the motion. The legs and hips really are doing the job here.

The mechanics for firing upper-cuts to the jaw or body are the same.

Rear uppercut
● The same mechanics as the lead uppercut. The shoulder aim is just slightly exaggerated to compensate for firing from the rear side.

Punching to the body

The mechanics for firing to the body are the same as firing to the head with one big difference. Use a bend of the knees (not a bend at the waist or you'll eat a knee) to take your punch into a horizontal plane with your target. And don't punch downhill (standing tall and punching in a downward trajectory). Punching downhill leaves your jaw completely exposed.

Jab to the body — good form

Jab to the body — not so much

No bend at knees plus downhill punching equals the above.

Bending at the waist invites the knee

Cross / rear straight to the body

Lead hook to the body

Rear hook to the body

Boxing Plus elbows

With all elbows we strike with the tip to cut, not to slam the forearm into the target. Elbows are not a power tool (although they do have power). They are precision cutting tools. Think of them as scalpels.

If you are close enough to throw an elbow, you are close enough to receive one. You must be defensively covered against an elbow when you throw your own. You can do this in one of two ways. Pick the one that feels right to you.

Cover elbow defense
● The on-guard arm is raised higher and held tighter to the head.

Palm cover elbow defense
● The on-guard hand is raised and the palm is turned to face your opponent, with the back of the hand placed on your head.

Palm cover in action next page.

Lead elbow
● With a relaxed loose hand, swing the elbow toward your target in a horizontal plane. No need to add waist torque to this.

Rear elbow
● The same mechanics.

Lead up elbow
● Use the standard elbow mechanics, but fire along the vertical plane.

Rear up elbow
● The same as the lead up elbow.

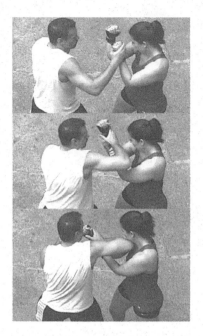

Lead scoop elbow
● The scoop elbow attempts to remove your opponent's on-guard hand on the way in.
● Throw your lead hand as if jabbing. You are actually attempting to land on the back of your opponent's hand or wrist.
● Pull/slap his hand/wrist away from his face and follow this pull/slap movement with your elbow in one simultaneous motion.

Rear scoop elbow
● The same mechanics.

4. Boxing Plus defensive vocabulary

This is a stripped down boxing defensive vocabulary, but in my opinion, it is not stripped down enough. Every defense offered below is completely viable and useful, but the vocabulary is a bit wider than needed.

Look at this way: Boxing Plus is basically six punches and four elbows. There is no need to make our defensive vocabulary more complex than the weapon coming at you.

There will be some defenses that work great for you and a little less for others. I would put each of these defenses through their paces in the focus mitt drills that we prescribe and allow your own reflexes and experience garnered in those rounds to make the decision as to what defenses to keep and what to throw away.

High jab defenses

Catch
● Receive the jab in the palm of the rear hand.
● Slap into it with a slight upward push.
● Don't reach for it (below).

Reaching for the jab exposes the head.

Inside cuff

● Use the palm of the rear hand on the outside of your opponent's wrist to slightly slap the punch to the inside.

● Rotating your palm to face you as you slap reduces your movement and gets you back to on-guard more rapidly than a muscular slap across the body.

Outside cuff

● Use the back of the rear hand or the outside of the wrist to direct the blow to the outside line.

Note the cuffing is just enough to redirect the punch without compromising defense.

Avoid a push and reach with the cuff hand. As shown, it leaves the head wide open to attack.

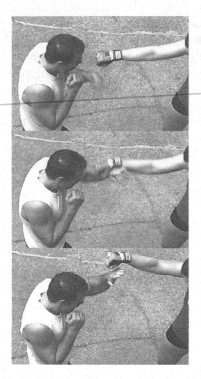

Up cuff
● Use the back of the hand to direct the punch to the upward line.

Lead muffle / stop

● Reach with the lead hand and cover the opponent's lead fist upon punch initiation or what you suspect is initiation.

Mark follows with the most natural of counters, a cross.

Rear muffle / stop

● Same as the preceding, but with the rear palm.

Cross glove
● This is a cuff performed with the lead hand.

Outside slip
● This is not a lateral lean.
● Hit a slight bend of the knees while …
● Turning the lead shoulder toward the rear knee allowing the punch to pass over your lead shoulder.
● Coach this motion by standing behind your fighter, if the butt bobs out or the fighter's upper body moves like a pendulum, that ain't right yet.

Pull
● This is a quick snap-back away from the punch.
● Use your stance pull and abs to bring you back into position immediately since this one leaves your lead leg a bit light.

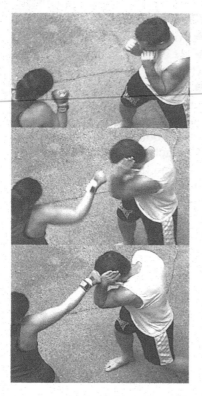

Lead cover

● Raise your rear guard and absorb the blow on the back of the hand/forearm.

● Not my favorite, but it has its place.

High cross defenses

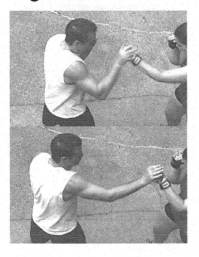

Catch
● The same mechanics as the jab catch, but this will require more slap as the cross is a stronger blow.

Cover
● The same mechanics as the jab cover. You'll find a slight bend of the knees upon impact acts as a sort of shock absorber.

Lead outside cuff
● Use the outside of your lead wrist to take the punch to the outside angle.

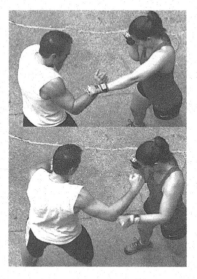

Lead inside cuff
● Use the lead hand to take the punch to the inside angle.

Mark follows up with a hook.

Cross glove
● Use the rear hand to cuff the punch to the outside angle.

Outside slip
● The same mechanics as the jab slip, but here you are going to the opposite side.

Pull

● The same as the jab pull.

Mark follows up with a cross.

Roll / shoulder block

● Not a go-to, but it has its place.

● Turn toward your inside line while folding the lead glove across your liver to protect against hooks.

● Raise your lead shoulder to protect your jaw.

● Bring your open glove (palm out) to reinforce your jaw protection.

Kylie follows up with a hook body, but her shot is blocked by the suggested defense.

High lead hook defenses

Cover
● You know what to do.

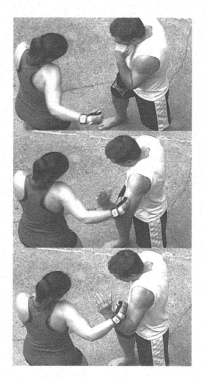

Forearm block
● Think of this as a loose cover.
● Use the forearm to block the incoming blow.

Duck
● Bend at the knees, not at the waist, to allow the punch to travel over you. Bend at the waist and say hello to a knee.

Cross glove catch
● Use the lead hand to catch the punch as your upper body fades from it just a bit.

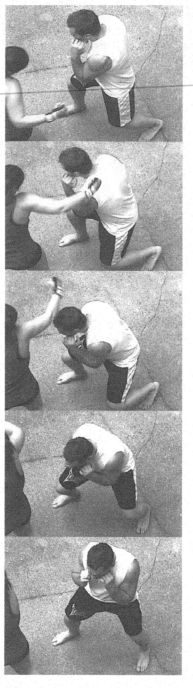

Bob & weave

● Execute a slip toward your inside.

● Stay low and turn the lead shoulder toward the rear knee coming up on the other side.

Note

High hooks can also be avoided with a pull. Although not pictured here, it's essentially the same as shown on page 52.

High rear hook defenses

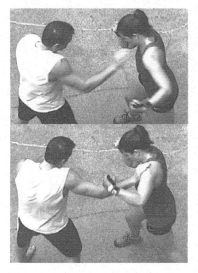

Shoulder stop
● Rear hooks are a little easier to read than lead hooks, and with a good eye, you can muffle them with a lead hand to the shoulder.

Biceps stop
● You can also use the lead hand to muffle on the biceps.

Forearm block

Cover

Duck

Uppercut defenses

Forearm blocks

● Keep your on-guard/forearms parallel position and with a slight turn of the waist, place an elbow/forearm in front of the blow.

Glove blocks

● You can also use a form of catch to stop these.
● Use the lead hand to chop downward into lead uppercuts and rear hand chops for rear uppercuts.

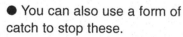

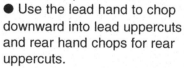

Pull

● A pull can also work for the uppercut angle.

Low jab defenses

Elbow block
● The same mechanics as the uppercut forearm block.

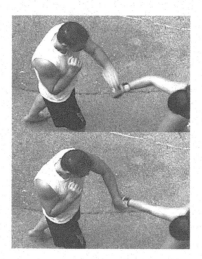

Outside scoop parry
● Use the lead hand to scoop/cuff the punch to the inside line.

Inside scoop
● Use the rear hand to scoop/cuff to the outside line.

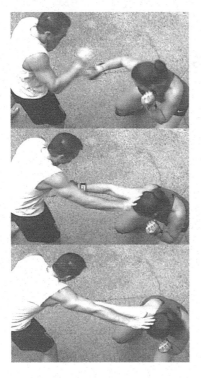

Post
● As you read that the blow is coming in ...
● Place the open lead glove on the head of your opponent as you fade the hips back placing him slightly out of range.

Low cross defenses

Elbow block

Lead scoop

Rear scoop

Low hook defenses

Forearm blocks

Blocking a lead hook ...

and blocking a rear hook.

Don't reach. Keep elbow in tight.   Mark pinches ideal target area.

Elbow defenses

Cover

● You can cover the same as you do for the hook angles with elbows.

Catch

● You can also catch them — right for right and left for left.

Up elbow defenses

Cover
● Treat these as you would the forearm block in the uppercut defense section.

5. Appetite for destruction

There is a class of defense that deserves to be discussed separately — a little tactic called destructions. Destructions are tactics (some would say dirty tactics) that damage the incoming blow (punches, kicks and knees). Old school pugilists were not above occasionally directing a defensive elbow into a punch to take a fist out, or at least give the opponent something to think about.

Filipino martial arts and Indonesian Silat systems took this idea a bit further in their approaches to kicks and knees. Some of these approaches can be a bit too baroque in execution to be practical, but a stripped-down approach can be mighty devastating. Witness Chris Weidman's horribly painful use of this tactic in his second bout with Anderson Silva. It still hurts me to see it. Here's to a speedy and full recovery Mr. Silva.

Destructions will not usually end with dire consequences (thankfully), but they can deliver enough sting to give the opponent second thoughts about particular blows or full power on a given technique.

Be advised of two things when training the destruction material:

1. No need to "hit" the incoming blow with your destruction defense, your opponent is supplying the damaging power by dint of his attack.

2. Train destruction defenses with care. These defenses can put a fist out of commission for a while so let's

play wisely. Full pads, 16 oz. gloves, shin guards, elbow pads, knee pads ... the whole bit. Along with an announcement that "Hey, this is a drill, so let's back down on the power."

Punch destructions

Cover point
Raise your arm versus straight punches as you would for a cover, but here attempt to direct the tip of your elbow into the incoming fist of your opponent.

Cuff point
● Raise your elbow as in the cover point, but here...
● You will use a secondary hand to cuff/guide the fist toward the elbow.

Kick covering & leg kick destructions

There are more than a few destructions for kicks to the head and body, but it is my opinion that they are a little less than practical. They often call for a guiding hand that leaves the defending forearm too exposed. Taking a full-on kick to a forearm or upper arm can result in a broken arm. With body and head kicks, let's play it safe and use the cover defense below (and/or the "Punch as cut-kick" strategy discussed later.)

Cover vs. body kick
● Treat it as you would a hook to the body.

Cover vs. straight kick to the body
● Treat it as you would an uppercut.

Bad form — elbow should be tight to body.

Cover vs. head kick

● Again, treat it as a hook.

Pull vs. straight kick to the head

Leg kick destructions

● Rather than checking the kick with shin-to-shin contact (not anterior tibialis contact which deadens the leg) ...

● Point the attacked leg into the incoming shin.

Knee destructions

Drop elbow
● As the knee rises to meet you, drop the tip of your elbow into the top of the thigh.

Cross elbow
● It is also possible to use standard elbow technique across the thigh to incur a bit of damage.

6. Punch, don't paw

There is a standard boxing maxim that says, "Half a punch is worse than no punch at all."

> **"Half a punch is worse than no punch at all."**

Sounds like some Zen koan advice given to Grasshopper in an episode of Kung Fu. What does "half a punch" even mean?

Well, (and get ready for an obvious statement) throwing punches is an energy exacting chore. Throwing lots of hard, strong punches can begin to feel an awful lot like work. But this work of throwing lots and lots of hard punches is what increases your odds of earning the KO or at least some solid damage points.

Back to that maxim, what exactly is half a punch?

If you will recall about every third fight you've seen in your life, there is often a display of one or both fighters throwing a combination or two in the air while both athletes are obviously out of each other's range. I'm not talking about throwing the jab as a probe, a range-finder or a reminder not to enter right now. I'm also not talking about feints and fakes. I'm talking about actual combinations thrown in the air, punches that have no chance of touching let alone solidly connecting with their presumably intended target. These are half punches.

Now, if throwing hard punches is energy exacting, throwing half punches also eats a bit of energy. Sure, not as much, but precious energy all the same. Energy that should be used on that live opponent right in front of you and not the atmosphere between the two of you.

Aside from wasting the precious resource of gas in the tank, I think throwing half punches is more damaging in another way. These air combos act as a sort of "Coming Attractions" preview, a little movie trailer of what is intended when fighters finally meet. You'll more often than not see the very same demonstration executed up close in the heat of battle. With that information in mind, a wise fighter (a wise corner) will make note of these half-punch displays and adjust their defense accordingly.

Let's look at another case study to have a look at a bout with a fighter who throws zero half punches.

Dial up UFC 167 and find the bout between Brian Ebersole and Rick Story. Ebersole is an excellent competitor with an entertainingly unorthodox approach and always a pleasure to watch. But this time I want you to watch Rick Story.

Rick, without ever winging his punches or failing to come back to good defensive position, *throws every single punch with absolute total commitment.* He is throwing every single punch with what Mike Tyson would call "bad intentions." Even when he misses the commitment is astonishing. When he makes contact it hurts me just to watch them land. Props to Ebersole for absorbing them as well as he did, but the lion's share of the props goes to Mr. Story for providing a lesson in what not "half-assing" it with half-punches looks like. Even on the ground and pound. Listen to the shots to the ribs and tell me you don't die a little inside when your hear that.

Thank you, Mr. Story for demonstrating the wisdom of the maxim.

7. Pyramid build

With all the focus pad drills, half of the heavy bag drills, half of our double-end bag drills, and with all of the partner flow drills, we will use the pyramid build to educate our skills. I'll pick an arbitrary combination to demonstrate how I want you to proceed through each drill.

Let's use the jab/cross/lead hook/rear uppercut (J/C/H/RU)

Assume you are going to work the heavy bag.

● Stand before the heavy bag just outside of range, step in and throw your jab, step back out immediately.
● Track the bag's movement and step in and throw your J/C combination then step out immediately.
● Track the bag's movement and step in to throw the J/C/H and step out.
● And finally step in to throw all four punches of the combination.
● Rinse, wash repeat.

By working in a pyramid build we front load the most important punches (the jab and the cross in this particular combination). Front loading means we have given them priority in the drill. Let's assume you make it through a total of 25 total builds of the given combination in the space of one round. In that one round you have thrown 25 iterations of the complete combination, but you have also thrown 100 jabs, 75 crosses and 50 lead hooks.

The pyramid build also provides you with mini-combinations inside larger combinations so you can counter staleness and begin multi-combination drilling from the get-go, thus increasing your volume (AKA swarming).

You will use the pyramid build in all drilling except the prescription scrimmage drills and half of the heavy bag and double-end bag drills.

Play it real
The number one most common error when doing any form of bag work is to treat the device like a toy and not a live opponent. In any gym you'll see fighters standing stock still, executing lazy punch recovery, dropping their hands and all sorts of rookie mistakes that wouldn't pass muster in the first round of a Golden Gloves junior division bout.

You've got to recall that "How you train is how you'll fight" maxim and give due diligence to treating the inanimate object in front of you like a bad intentioned opponent. I know, it's easy to fall into a playtime pattern, but let's keep it real by playing it like it is real.

Let's get heavy
Use the heavy bag to build Power with a capital **P**. We don't want to push the bag, we don't want to shove the bag. We want to snap into that bag and hone our mechanics until we find the timing to make every shot pack a wallop.

With this program we provide two ways to approach the bag. The first was mentioned earlier.

In-out pyramid build *(see page 81)*

● First, we select our combination. Here we use the J/C/H/RU.
● Stand just outside of punching range (pretend that bag can smack back).
● Step in and fire that jab for all your worth and then step out.
● Allow the bag to swing, don't steady it. We want to learn to track movement and how to increase power by meeting incoming mass creating a fistic head-on collision.
● Step back in and fire the J/C. Step out.
● And so on and so forth.
● Once you've fired all four punches, restart the pyramid build and continue in this fashion until the round is over.

Keep it up!

No cheating.

Out-of-plumb turnover

● We still want some power, but it is not the primary goal — we're building punching stamina.
● We will take our root combination from the prior drill and instead of stair-stepping it through the pyramid, we will execute the J/C/H/RU as one continuous loop until the round is over.
● You got that? Don't stop punching.
● Your goal is to stay tight on the bag throwing short choppy shots that keep the bag just out of vertical plumb.
● You can't shove into the bag or use your head to keep it out of plumb. It must stay out of the vertical plane by dint of your rapid punch turnover.
● Enjoy the burn!

Double duty on the double-end bag

Just as with the heavy bag, the double-end bag has a twofold drill approach in this program. The first is the standard pyramid build, but there is a difference on the double-end bag.

● You won't build power, but you will build some eye-hand coordination.
● Also, I want you to stay on top of the bag, no in and out.
● We want to stay close enough and punch just hard enough that the bag provides some snap-back allowing us to work some of our upper-body mobility (pulls and slips).

We also use the punch turnover, but there is no bag to get out of plumb. Simply use your given combination in a continuous loop and keep that bag snapping and popping until the round is over.

Pyramid build

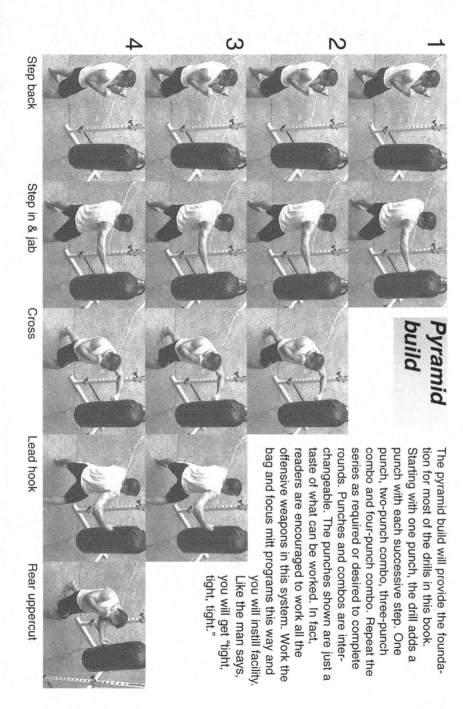

1 Step back

2 Step in & jab

3 Cross

4 Lead hook

Rear uppercut

The pyramid build will provide the foundation for most of the drills in this book. Starting with one punch, the drill adds a punch with each successive step. One punch, two-punch combo, three-punch combo and four-punch combo. Repeat the series as required or desired to complete rounds. Punches and combos are interchangeable. The punches shown are just a taste of what can be worked. In fact, readers are encouraged to work all the offensive weapons in this system. Work the bag and focus mitt programs this way and you will instill facility. Like the man says, you will get "tight, tight, tight."

8. Let's stay focused

Food for thought for feeders

One of the most useful pieces of gear for building your boxing base are focus pads, AKA focus mitts. Focus pads in the hands of a good trainer (also known as the feeder) will allow you to build power, speed, offense, defense, footwork, strategy, tactics and beaucoup other corollary attributes. But the key to building these attributes is intelligent use of the pads. Merely having a friend don them and you smacking at them willy-nilly is not really the way to build your skills. Using focus pads without a plan is simply asking your partner to indulge you as a not quite heavy enough heavy bag. To use focus pads you need focus.

Good form. Target pad is face out in front of shoulder and chest. Mark's pad meets Kylie's punch with resistance. The pad not in use is turned in.

Intelligent focus pad use requires two savvy partners — a good feeder who is actually providing what is to be focused upon, and an athlete who must focus on what is being fed to him.

Being a good feeder

● Keep the pads close to the targets to be hit — optimally positioned somewhat in front of the shoulders or chest. There's nothing worse than a feeder holding pads wide apart. This encourages the fighter to punch wide. Very bad.

Above the feeder's pads are too far apart. This trains wide punching. No good.

Don't let the punch blow you back. Feeder must offer resistance with a slap into the punch.

Combination with focus pads.

Jab

Cross

Lead hook

Rear hook

● The feeder chooses when the pad is to be hit, the fighter has no say in it. Keep those pads facing inward toward your chest, or facing one another and flash the targets and angles you want when it's time to hit. Don't be the feeder who just leaves the face of the pads exposed at all times allowing the fighter to hit whenever he likes. If you're too lazy to feed correctly, do your fighter a kindness and send him to the heavy bag where at least there's an excuse to be inanimate.

● Smack back into the punch you are feeding. Don't simply allow the punch to blow your hand away. You must give short sharp smacks into the fed punch so that your partner has some resistance and learns to feel that bite. This smack back also allows the feeder quicker rebound into the next position.

● Be active. Heavy bags hang more or less in a vertical plane, the same with the double-end bag. If you are feeding you need to be on the move. One of the huge benefits of proper focus pad work is building offensive and defensive footwork and upper body movement that the aforementioned two pieces of gear simply can't provide.

● Have a plan. Sure, sometimes it's fun just to feed random targets and angles and that sort of free form is a nice way to polish off a session. But intelligent use of the focus pads requires you to pick an attribute (or set of attributes) to work on in that session and utilize drills to hone the skills you want to see sharpened.

Feed positions

The rule is right for right and left for left. In other words, I feed the my right mitt to get a right-handed punch from my athlete, and a left mitt feed for a left-hand punch.

Jab feed
● Mitt is held high approximately 10-12 inches from the fed target (here the head).

Cross feed
● Flip the preceding tip.

High hooks
● The mitt is held vertically just in front of the designated target.

Uppercuts
● Feed the mitt horizontally.

For body shots don a belly-pad. Low mitt feeds start losing their smack-back power and it gets tougher to feed your athlete a true angle.

Focus mitt drills

OK, now that we know what's expected of a good feeder, let's give the feeder a tiered drill set to build these intelligent skills we've been talking about.

Ideally you will put every single combination in the combination menus through each of these drills, giving each combination and individual drill at least a single 3-5 minute round. We will pick one combination and demonstrate it throughout all of the drills. We will use J/C/H/RU.

No pressure pyramid
● Use the pyramid method to walk through the pyramid, feeling the combination with no onus on the feeder or the fighter to be creative or on the go. Simply find your feed and your punches.

In & out pyramid
● Here the fighter will start just outside of range. When he sees the pad flashed, he steps in and punches and then moves out immediately.
● He must step in at the start of each feed and step out after each pyramid build.
● It is important to keep your weight underneath you and not to fall into your punches or overload the lead foot. Learn to be light.

The next four drills will educate how to bang on the move toward all the primary compass points, as well as educate a pivot versus an advance.

1. Advancing pyramid (See next page)
● The feeder will step back and flash the pad.
● The fighter steps forward and bangs the jab.
● The feeder steps back and flashes for the 1-2 and so on.

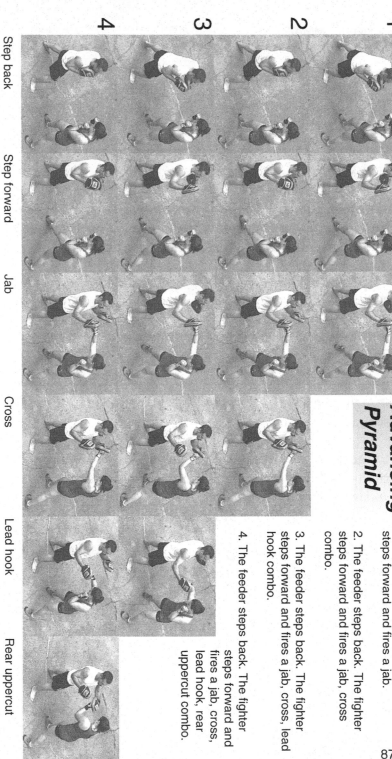

1 Step back

2 Step forward

3 Jab

4 Cross

Lead hook

Rear uppercut

Advancing Pyramid

1. The feeder steps back. The fighter steps forward and fires a jab.

2. The feeder steps back. The fighter steps forward and fires a jab, cross combo.

3. The feeder steps back. The fighter steps forward and fires a jab, cross, lead hook combo.

4. The feeder steps back. The fighter steps forward and fires a jab, cross, lead hook, rear uppercut combo.

87

A little digression for the spear

There is often a tendency in beginner feeders to simply feed the drill again and again straight down the gym in a linear manner. Meaning, "OK, we've just completed the pyramid, let's start again from where we're standing."

There's nothing necessarily wrong with that, but I find that providing a little mental reset/pause for your athlete is a wiser way to go. We don't want this pause to be passive, so ...

● At the end of each pyramid build, pull one of your mitts to your face.
● Extend the other mitt in front of you as if you've frozen a jab or rear straight at the end.
● Walk forward directly into your fighter.
● He/she will have to pivot/side step to avoid your advance.
● At that point we will consider the fighter reset and you restart your pyramid build.

I urge you not to hedge your spear — aim that mitt right for the nose and walk into them. I want you to spear after each pyramid completion on every single mitt drill that calls for movement.

2. Retreating pyramid
● The feeder steps forward and feeds the jab.
● The fighter steps back and fires the jab.
● Do not hit as you move, but after your stance is set. This may seem like a distinction without a difference, but once you find the "feel" of it, you'll be happy you were disciplined.
● Continue the build.

3. Outside lateral pyramid
● The feeder steps laterally toward his fighter's back — away

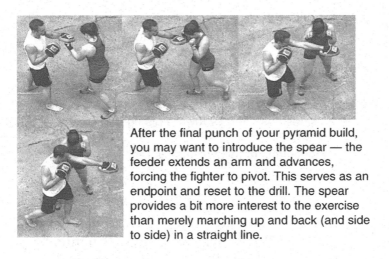

After the final punch of your pyramid build, you may want to introduce the spear — the feeder extends an arm and advances, forcing the fighter to pivot. This serves as an endpoint and reset to the drill. The spear provides a bit more interest to the exercise than merely marching up and back (and side to side) in a straight line.

Retreating pyramids have the feeder stepping forward and the fighter taking a step back before punching.

Lateral pyramids (traveling right or left) have the feeder sidestepping and the fighter following with her own sidestep before punching.

from the power hand — and feeds the jab.
● The fighter side steps to follow, gets his feet under him and fires the jab.
● Continue the build.

4. Inside lateral pyramid
● The feeder sidesteps laterally toward his fighter's chest — he then feeds the jab.
● The fighter sidesteps to follow, gets his feet under him and fires.
● Continue the build.

The next four drills will add to the movement and pivot theme. Here the feeder will "draw" his fighter. By drawing I mean you use a bit of baiting footwork to lure/draw the fighter toward you and then meet him with a head-on collision.

1. Advancing +1 (cross)
● The feeder steps back and feeds the jab.
● The fighter steps forward and fires the jab.
● All is the same as the advancing pyramid until after the last punch.
● The feeder skips the spear ...
● The fighter steps back one step after his last punch.
● The feeder steps forward one step and feeds the cross.
● The fighter steps forward one step to meet the feeder's advance and bangs the cross.
● The feeder shoots the spear and the fighter pivots for the reset.

2. Retreating +1 (cross)
3. Outside +1 (cross)
4. Inside +1 (cross)

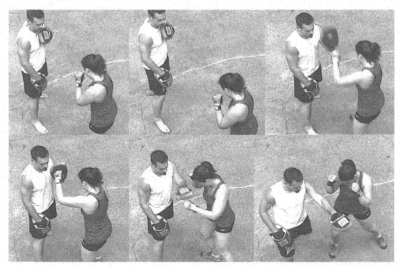

+ 1 (cross)
After the pyramid, the fighter steps back, drawing the feeder. The fighter throws a cross. The feeder shoots a spear that the fighter pivots to avoid.

+ 1 (lead hook)
Same as above except the fighter throws a lead left hook.

We will now run another +1 drawing drill set that is essentially the same as the last series, but here instead of your +1 shot being a cross, it's a lead hook.

1. Advancing + 1 (lead hook)
2. Retreating +1 (lead hook)
3. Outside +1 (lead hook)
4. Inside +1 (lead hook)

The next four drills train your fighter to execute head movement before each punch. In these four drills we will use a slip.

1. Advancing poke & go #1
● The feeder steps back.
● The fighter follows.
● The feeder fires a jab at the fighter's head.
● The fighter slips outside and fires the jab.
● Continue the build with the jab to inside slip being at the top of each step of the way and, as always, followed by the spear/pivot/reset at the end of the build.

2. Retreating poke & go #1
3. Outside poke & go #1
4. Inside poke & go #1

The next four drills continue the head-movement theme, but here the feeder is firing a rear straight at the head for the fighter to outside slip on the opposite side.

1. Advancing poke & go #2
2. Retreating poke & go #2
3. Outside poke & go #2
4. Inside poke & go #2

Poke & go #1
The feeder throws a jab, the fighter slips outside and counters with a jab.

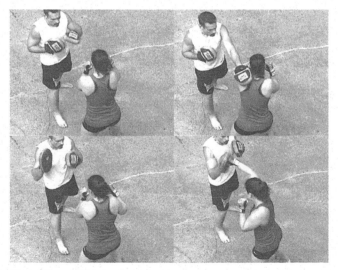

Poke & go #2
The feeder throws a rear straight, the fighter slips outside and counters with a jab.

The next four drills educate more upper-body movement with the bob-and-weave being the focus here. Note that if you've been diligent about following these drills in the prescribed order your footwork with the given combination probably feels golden by now.

Side bar
You can take any defense for the straight punches and plug them into the poke & go series. As a matter of fact, I heartily encourage this.

For example, rather than execute an inside slip each time with poke & go drill #1, you can cross glove, and so on.

1. Advancing swing & a miss #1
● Use the root combination and build as usual.
● After the last punch is thrown the feeder swings a wide lead hook to the fighter's head.
● The fighter bobs-and-weaves (inside to outside) and returns a C/H combination.
● The feeder spears for the reset.

2. Retreating swing & a miss #1
3. Outside swing & a miss #1
4. Inside swing & a miss #1

Avoid detouring ...   veering ...   and chopping.

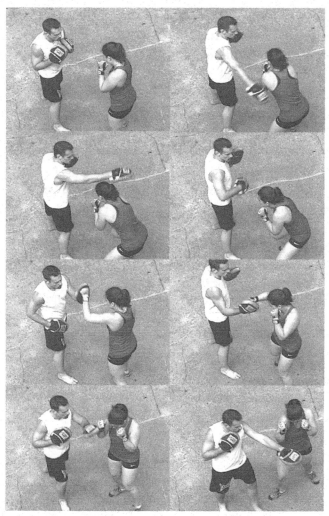

Swing & a miss #1

Perfect.

The next four drills build the bob-and-weave from the opposite side and introduce the use of the belly pad, which allows the fighter to bang to the body without awkward mitt angles that provide little resistance.

Adding the belly pad

The next two versions of swing and a miss require the feeder to strap on a belly pad. Belly pads are ideal tools to build working body shots without your fighter having to pull his punches or feed inauthentic angles with the mitts that won't allow for good power build.

1. Advancing swing & a miss #2
● After the last punch of the root combination is fired, the feeder gives a wide rear hook to the head.
● The fighter bobs-and-weaves (inside to outside) and fires a RHB/LHB.
● The feeder spears for the reset.

2. Retreating swing & a miss #2
3. Outside swing & a miss #2
4. Inside swing & a miss #2

Swing & a miss #2

Here's one more swing & a miss variation.

1. Advancing swing & a miss #3
● This time the feeder will swing a lead hook again after the last punch of the root combo.
● The fighter bobs-and-weaves (inside to outside) and returns a HB/RHB.
● The feeder spears for the reset.

2. Retreating swing & a miss #3
3. Inside swing & a miss #3
4. Outside swing & a miss #3

Swing & a miss #3

1. Advancing cutting the uppercut #1
● After the root combination, the feeder fires a lead uppercut.
● The fighter covers with the rear forearm and returns a lead hook.

2. Retreating cutting the uppercut #1
3. Inside cutting the uppercut #1
4. Outside cutting the uppercut #1

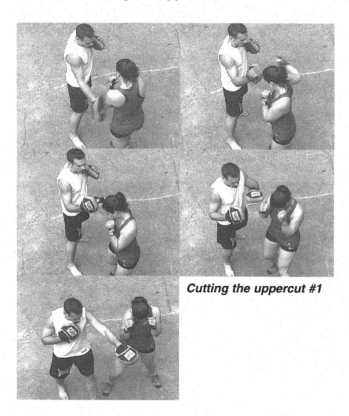

Cutting the uppercut #1

1. Advancing cutting the uppercut #2
● Here the feeder fires a rear uppercut.
● The fighter covers with a rear forearm and fires a cross/hook.

2. Retreating cutting the uppercut #2
3. Inside cutting the uppercut #2
4. Outside cutting the uppercut #2

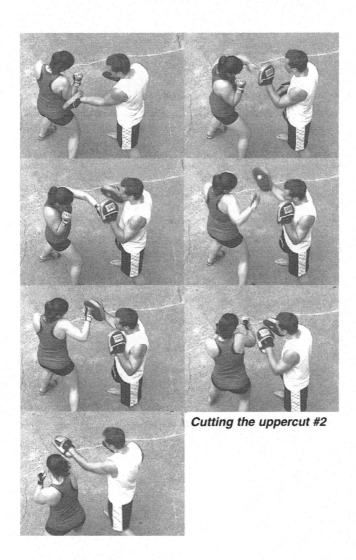

Cutting the uppercut #2

1. Advancing elbow for elbow #1
● Here the feeder fires a lead elbow after the root combo.
● The feeder catches with the lead hand and...
● Returns a rear elbow.

2. Retreating elbow for elbow #1
3. Inside elbow for elbow #1
4. Outside elbow for elbow #1

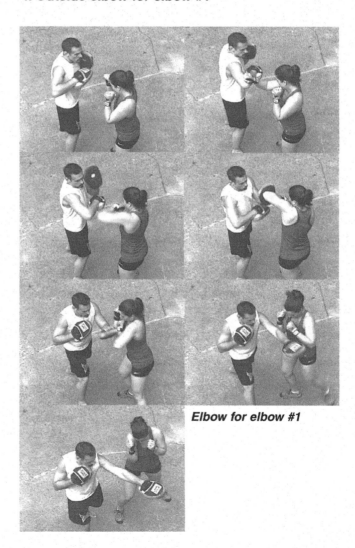

Elbow for elbow #1

1. Advancing elbow for elbow #2
● The feeder fires a rear elbow.
● The fighter catches with the rear hand and fires a lead elbow.

2. Retreating elbow for elbow #2
3. Inside elbow for elbow #2
4. Outside elbow for elbow #2

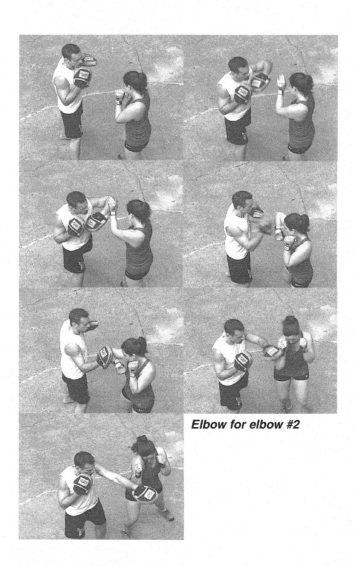

Elbow for elbow #2

1. Advancing elbow for elbow #3
● Here the feeder fires a lead up elbow after the root combo.
● The feeder blocks with the rear forearm and...
● Returns a lead up elbow/rear elbow combination.

2. Retreating elbow for elbow #3
3. Inside elbow for elbow #3
4. Outside elbow for elbow #3

Elbow for elbow #3

1. Advancing elbow for elbow #4

● Here the feeder fires a rear up elbow after the root combo.
● The feeder blocks with the lead forearm and...
● Returns a rear up elbow/lead elbow combination.

2. Retreating elbow for elbow #4
3. Inside elbow for elbow #4
4. Outside elbow for elbow #4

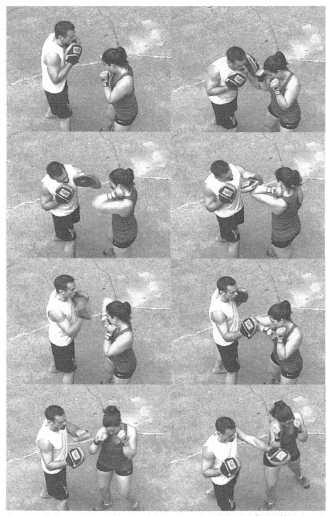

Elbow for elbow #4

1. Advancing cover point #1
● Think of this as a poke & go #1 variant.
● The feeder fires a jab at the start of each feed.
● The fighter offers a rear cover point destruction as he works through the root combination.

2. Retreating cover point #1
3. Inside cover point #1
4. Outside cover point #1

... and so on with the remaining combos in the pyramid build.

1. Advancing cover point #2
● Think of this as a poke & go #2 variant.
● The feeder fires a cross at the start of each feed.
● The fighter offers a lead cover point destruction as he works through the root combination.

2. Retreating cover point #2
3. Inside cover point #2
4. Outside cover point #2

1. Advancing cuff point #1
● Think of this as another poke & go #1 variant.
● The feeder fires a jab at the start of each feed.
● The fighter offers lead hand cuff to rear destruction as he works through the root combination.

2. Retreating cuff point #1
3. Inside cuff point #1
4. Outside cuff point #1

1. Advancing cuff point #2
● Think of this as another poke & go #2 variant.
● The feeder fires a cross at the start of each feed.
● The fighter offers uses a rear hand cuff to lead destruction as he works through the root combination.

2. Retreating cuff point #1
3. Inside cuff point #1
4. Outside cuff point #1

1. Advancing sprawl & get-up
● After the last punch of your root combination the feeder will shoot the takedown.
● The fighter will sprawl, hip post and hit a proper stand-up.

2. Retreating sprawl & get-up
3. Inside sprawl & get-up
4. Outside sprawl & get-up

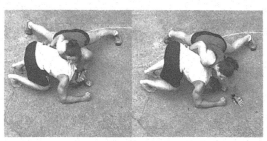

Pushing straight down on his head will enable him to get up.

Sprawl & get-up

Push down and away
to ensure your
escape.

Sidebar

You can plug any defense against a hook into the swing & a miss drills and/or the feeder can substitute uppercuts where the swing is prescribed to educate the fighter defending and responding to this attack angle.

After you've run a root combination though all of these drills, you'll be focused and tight, tight, tight! You can pick the next combination and get to work, remembering to use the belly pad when you have any body shots in the root combination.

And/or ...

You can blend the drills. For example, open the pyramid with a poke & go #1 and end it with a +1, or a swing & a miss. I recommend not hitting blends until the root combination of choice has been shot through all of the prescribed permutations top to bottom.

I think between the combination menu and the focus mitt drills, you'll be punching and moving sharper than you ever imagined.

9. No hitting below the belt ... Why not?

Boxing has a strict no blows below the belt rule that we all take to mean no shots to the groin, but you'll also notice this forbids punching the thighs and hips. MMA has a low blow rule as well, but it applies to only groin shots. If you stay away from the cup and its surrounding neighborhood, it's all legal. Admittedly, most of the strikes delivered below the belt come via kicks and knees, but you are seeing a slowly growing minority of fighters who are punching and hammer-fisting thighs.

Punching the legs lacks the definitive "oomph" of a leg kick or knee strike, but it is still a strike all the same and can render a bit of damage in two senses. First, any strike to your opponent's body is a good thing. While not as punishing as a leg kick or a knee, a good punch or hammerfist can still "frog" the fatigued quadriceps.

Secondly, it's a bit discombobulating. Attempting to block what he thought was a low jab to the body that turned into a stiff straight to the thigh, gives an opponent more to ponder than he might have initially realized. Placing more weapons and targets on the table is always a good thing.

You've got a couple of ways to go with boxing the legs — out-range work and clinch work. Below are a few combinations for each contingency so you can begin incorporating this unusual but effective approach into your training.

Boxing the legs out-range combination

Essentially any punch that is delivered to the body can be drifted to the legs with the exception of uppercuts. Drifting an uppercut this low provides too much countering surface area. The half dozen combinations on the next two pages will get you going with the concept.

After you have these under your belt, so to speak, head over to the combination menu and work on making these other low-shot-included combinations just as facile.

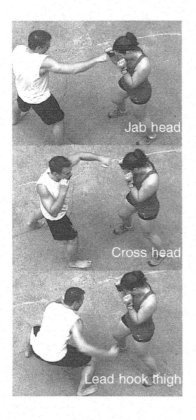

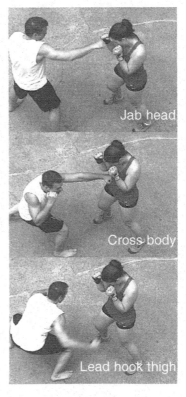

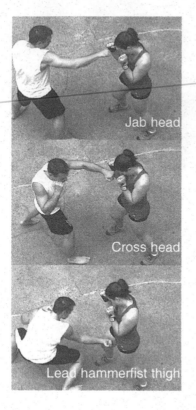

Jab head

Lead hammerfist thigh

Cross head

Cross body

Lead hammerfist thigh

Boxing the legs clinch combinations

Boxing the legs inside the clinch is more along the line of insert shots, meaning taking single and/or double shot opportunities as they come. The nature of the clinch does not permit high number combination work. Pictured on the next page are a number of suitable punches.

They can yield these combinations:

Lead hook outside of thigh/
Lead hammerfist inside of thigh

Rear hook outside of thigh/
Rear hammerfist inside of thigh

Lead hammerfist inside of thigh/
Lead hook outside of thigh

Rear hammerfist inside of thigh/
Rear hook outside of thigh

Lead hammerfist outside of thigh

Lead hook outside of thigh

Lead hammerfist inside of thigh

Lead hook inside of thigh

Rear hammerfist outside of thigh

Rear hook outside of thigh

Rear hammerfist inside of thigh

Rear hook inside of thigh

117

10. Sunday punch as cut-kick

In the devastating sport of Muay Thai there is an advanced strategy to counter the kick called cut-kicking. Cut-kicking, essentially requires you to time firing your own kick to your opponent's support leg as his kick is coming in. It's a tricky strategy that calls for good reflexes and sharp timing, but it's not a bad skill to have.

I think we can save time learning to cut-kick by substituting a step-in plus a Sunday punch which stands in the cut-kick's stead. This was a very useful approach we saw being coached by the late great Shawn Tompkins, and we have a beautiful example of it in UFC 102 in the bout between Nate Marquardt and Demian Maia.

Go ahead and dial up the fight, but don't blink.

Now that you've had a look, you have an idea of what we have in mind here.

First things, first. A Thai kick, whether it be to the leg, body or head is a formidable weapon to see coming at you, and it is mighty wise to take some stink off its power. There are two ways to do this, one obvious and the other counter intuitive. The obvious answer is to step away or evade. The other is to step *into* the kick. Both strategies are utilizing essentially the same leverage principles to varying degrees, but only one leaves you in countering range (the second).

Think of the kick as a ball bat, with the foot being the striking end of the bat and the hips being where the bat is gripped. The optimum striking surface of this ball bat is the shin. To take power from this ball bat we either need to move beyond the tip of the bat (strategy #1) or step closer to where the bat is gripped (the hips). Both strategies are utilizing the concept of moving away from the optimum power surface (the shin). The step-in method places you in good countering position and in a far less powerful striking zone. You are also in the enviable position of being a two-legged fighter striking a one-legged fighter.

With the above in mind, let's address drills to begin educating the Sunday punch as cut-kick. Insert these drills at the end of a focus pad root combination in the format of a swing & a miss.

Interrupting the leg kick #1
● After the root combination, the feeder fires a leg kick (rear or inside).
● The fighter steps in and fires a cross.

Interrupting the body kick #1

● Same drill, but the kick is fired to the body.

Interrupting the head kick #1

Interrupting the leg kick #2

● Here the fighter returns a lead hook to the head.

Interrupting the body kick #2

Interrupting the head kick #2

An alternate strategy for the step-in and interrupt, where the punch and step-in are almost simultaneous, is to step-in while covering versus the kick and then firing your counter.

Step-in & cover vs. leg kick #1

● The return fire will be the cross on each of these.

Step-in & cover vs. body kick #1

Step-in & cover vs. head kick #1

Step-in & cover vs. leg kick #2
● Here the return fire after the step-in and cover is a lead hook to the head.

Step-in & cover vs. body kick #2

Step-in & cover vs. head kick #2

11. Boxing Plus sprawl & get-up

We'd be a little less than remiss if we did not address the takedown. That is, defending against it. After all, this is MMA, not straight boxing. We have addressed takedown defense in prior volumes, but here we're going to cut that vocabulary to the bare bones and assume that you want to stay on your feet.

In making this assumption there are two caveats. First, let's not assume that one takedown defense is all you'll need. Far from it. But a good sprawl can go a long, long way to curing what ails you 80-90 percent of the time.

Second, if you don't want to go back to your feet and you still want to strike (which is a mighty good strategy, our book *No Holds Barred Fighting: The Book of Essential Submissions* details how more fights are won via ground and pound than via submissions) pick up our book *MMA Mastery: Ground and Pound* for an in-depth treatment of this topic.

But again, here we will present one idea, just one — the almighty sprawl. The sprawl is your go-to takedown defense in most circumstances, so if we're going to need a sprawl (and we all do) let's do it right.

1. Hit your opponent with your hips, not your chest. Laying your chest on your opponent is an easy way for your opponent to complete that takedown.

2. Get convex. Look to the sky, push those hips through in the most vulgar manner you can manage, arch that spine and don't stop until you know you're safe. Looking down and/or leaning forward will make your hips lighter on your opponent and the takedown will be completed.

3. Throw those feet back. You can't sprawl and remain standing at the same time.

4. If you want the fight to get back to the feet, grab nothing. There is a huge temptation to overhook or underhook a head, a shoulder, an arm or the waist (bad call, that). If you want the fight to get back to the feet, sprawl and post both hands on your opponent's hips and push them away.

5. Stand up correctly. To stand up from a sprawl ...

● Pick a side you want to stand up on. Here we're standing up to our left — the opponent's right.

● Leave your left hand hip post in play.

● Post your right hand on the back of your opponent's head and drive it away (not down).

● Push with both hands to get to the feet.

Let's not work the sprawl and get-up in isolation, let's mix it from the beginning. Going back to our focus mitt drills, use it as a swing & a miss insert.

● After the last punch of your root combination, the feeder will shoot the takedown.

● The fighter will sprawl, hip post and hit a proper stand-up.

● Take the drill through all forms — advancing, retreating, moving inside and outside.

This one simple drill added to your focus mitt matrix should make you good to go.

12. Combination menus

The following combinations are understood to be shot through all forms of the previously described drills. Sure, you can skip around to pick and choose combos that fit your needs, but I heartily suggest once you pick a combo to run it through the drill matrix top to bottom for some serious Boxing Plus fluidity.

Legend
J = Jab
C = Cross or rear straight
H = Lead hook
RH = Rear hook
LU = Lead uppercut
RU = Rear uppercut
O = Overhand
LE = Lead elbow
RE = Rear elbow
LUE = Lead up elbow
RUE = Rear up elbow

No designation means the strike is delivered to the head (chin, eye, nose, whatever's open).

Any shot to the body will be designated by the capital letter B as in JB, which is to be read as jab to the body.

Any combination that changes levels from body to head will use a capital H to mean a return to the Head, so J/CB/HH should be read as jab head/cross body/hook head.

Now that that's clear as mud, here are 82 combinations to run through all drill templates.

Two-point combinations
Double jab
JH/JB
JB/JH
Double jab body
J/C
JH/CB
JB/CH
JB/CB
J/H
JB/HH
JB/RHH
JH/JB/C
J/LU
J/RU
LU/J
C/H
CB/HH
CH/HB
Double lead hook
● Bang the first hook to the body.
● Pull the lead hand just a bit without a return to face and then bang the head.
Double rear hook — low to high
● See the preceding note.
H/LU
H/CB
RU/H
LU/RH
LU/RU
RU/H
RU/C
RU/J
H/R

H/RU
RH/RU
RU/RH

Three-point combinations
Triple jab
J/H/LU
J/LU/H
J/J/C
JH/JB/HH
J/C/H
J/C/LU
J/H/RH
C/H/C
H/C/H
H/LU/C
H/LU/RH
HB/HH/RU
J/CB/HH
J/C/J
J/RU/H
J/H/C
J/H/RU
J/HB/H
J/LU/RH
LU/RH/H

Four-point combinations
J/C/HB/RU
C/H/C/HB
C/H/CB/LU
J/H/C/H
J/HB/HH/RU
J/CB/H/RHB

H/RH/LU/RU
LU/H/RU/RH
H/LU/RH/RU
H/RU/LU/RH

Five-point combinations
J/C/LU/C/H
H/C/LU/RH/HB
J/J/C/H/C

Six-point combinations
J/C/H/C/LU/RU
J/C/LU/C/H/RU

Boxing Plus combinations

2-point combinations
J/RE
C/LE
CB/LUE
H/RE
J/LE

Three-point combinations
J/C/LE
J/LE/RE
C/H/RE
C/RE/C
J/C/LUE
C/LUE/RE
RU/H/RE
C/HB/RE
HB/RE/LUE

13. Prescription for scrimmage drills

Sparring can be a delicate balancing act. Some fighters look good during training drills, but the jitters of the scrimmage bollixes up their skills. Others view sparring as an actual fight (which it is not) and take it too far.

Sparring is in some respects a fight, but it is a controlled fight. One with specific skills to be highlighted and reinforced.

To help get the jittery fighter under control and to reign in the "In it to win it!" fighter, I suggest using the following scrimmage forms to help build the sparring game. Once fighters of both classes and all those in between have worked through these templates, the jittery fighter should be calmed and the brawler reigned in. Both fighters will have honed some real-time movement.

All footwork, upper-body work and defense is at play in each of these drills.

One-for-one body killer
● Both fighters can only throw one blow at a time with the body being the only allowable target.

One-for-one head hunting
● Same one-for-one format with the head being the target of choice.

One-for-one body killer vs. head hunter
● One fighter bangs to the body, the other to the head.
● Switch roles with alternating rounds.

One-for-one full body
● The head and the body are allowable targets.

One-for-one counter the leader
● Fighter A always starts the punch initiation.
● Fighter B can only fire a shot as Fighter A's is coming in.
● Switch roles with alternating rounds.

One-for-one phone booth
● Chalk off a 5-foot square and scrimmage in this cut-off ring.

One-for-one super glue
● Here's a chance to work on shelling up and working upper-body movement.
● Both fighters hit their stance just inside punching range.
● Do not move your feet — no stepping, no picking them up.

One-for-one fox & hound
● Fighter A utilizes the whole ring or octagon hitting on the move.
● Fighter B must stalk him and attempt to cut the ring off.
● Switch roles with alternating rounds.

One-for-one general vs. cage drive
● Fighter A wants to maintain the center of the ring/octagon at all costs — spinning back to center in all circumstances.
● Fighter B wants to drive him to the ropes or cage and pin him there.
● Switch roles with alternating rounds.

One-for-one all D vs. all O
● Fighter A is a punching bag on the move using nothing but evasion and defense to survive the round.
● Fighter B stalks and lands.
● Switch roles with alternating rounds.

One-for-one southpaw
● Fighter A assumes the Southpaw role.
● Fighter B the orthodox boxer.
● Switch roles with alternating rounds.

One-for-one boxer vs. Boxer Plus
● Fighter A uses only his boxing arsenal.
● Fighter B uses Boxing Plus.
● Switch roles with alternating rounds.

One-for-one boxer vs. kick-boxer
● Fighter A uses only the boxing arsenal.
● Fighter B can use boxing and kicking—kicks should be emphasized in this drill template.
● Switch roles with alternating rounds.

Run all prior drills through two-for-two and two-for-one iterations and then you and/or your fighters will be up to full sparring in no time.

Take care of the noggin

Boxing and MMA are contact sports. If you train and play up to speed, there will be repeated blows to the head. Here are a few ways to get the most out of your Boxing Plus program without sacrificing cognitive function down the road.

1. Obey the rules of safety and gear up appropriately, please. This means mandatory mouthpiece, headgear and sparring gloves (not MMA gloves) whether you're training with head contact that day or not.

2. Reduce contact training to the head to no more than once every 10 days (if even that much). Don't think you're missing out, there's more than a few fighters including (current of this writing) UFC welterweight champ Johny Hendricks who takes zero shots to the head at all in his training, and he seems to respond to head shots, and throws hands to the head inside the Octagon just fine.

3. Let your bag training and focus mitt work fill in for actual human heads more often than not.

4. If you are going to include head shots in your training, by all means reduce the contact. There's no need to bang the skull like you dig to the body — you're sparring, you're training —let it loose during the fight.

In short, please consider following Johny Hendricks lead. As long as you adhere to all other aspects of the drill hierarchy, you should be good to go and avoid needless headaches and worse.

Conclusion

Well, that's all she wrote for this volume. I sincerely hope you find the logical, linear, pragmatic drill template provided within these pages a serious boon for your Boxing Plus program.

For further drills and/or questions, visit our site www.extremeselfprotection.com I always love hearing from you folks and how your progress is going.

Until I hear from you...Train hard, Train safely, and may you experience much success with your Boxing Plus Program.

Mark Hatmaker

Resources

BEST CHOICES
First, please visit my website at
www.extremeselfprotection.com
You will find even more training
material as well as updates and
other resources.

Amazon.com
The place to browse for books such
as this one and other similar titles.

Paladin Press
www.paladin-press.com
Paladin carries many training
resources as well as some of my
videos, which allow you to see
much of what is covered in my
NHB books.

Ringside Boxing
www.ringside.com
Best choice for primo equipment.

Sherdog.com
Best resource for MMA news, event
results and NHB happenings.

Threat Response Solutions
www.trsdirect.com
They also offer many training
resources along with some of my
products.

Tracks Publishing
www.trackspublishing.com
They publish all the books in the
NHBF series and MMA series as
well as a few fine boxing titles.

www.humankinetics.com
Training and conditioning info.

www.matsmatsmats.com
Best resource for quality mats at
good prices.

Video instruction

Extreme Self-Protection
extremeselfprotection.com

Paladin Press
paladin-press.com

Threat Response Solutions
trsdirect.com

World Martial Arts
groundfighter.com

Events

IFC
ifc-usa.com

IVC
valetudo.com

King of the Cage
kingofthecage.com

Pancrase
so-net.ne.jp/pancrase

Pride
pridefc.com

The Ultimate Fighting
Championships
ufc.tv

Universal Combat Challenge
ucczone.ca/

Index

Books by Mark Hatmaker

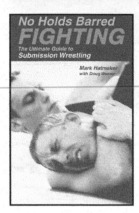

**No Holds Barred Fighting:
The Ultimate Guide
to Submission Wrestling**
The combat art of The Ultimate Fighting
Championships.
978-1-884654-17-6 / $12.95
695 photos

**More No Holds Barred Fighting:
Killer Submissions**
More takedowns, rides and submissions
from the authors of *No Holds Barred
Fighting.*
978-1-884654-18-3 / $12.95
650 photos

**No Holds Barred Fighting:
Savage Strikes**
*The Complete Guide to Real World
Striking for NHB Competition
and Street Defense*
Punches, kicks, forearm shots, head
butts and more.
978-1-884654-20-6 / $12.95
850 photos

Boxing Mastery
*Advance Techniques, Tactics and
Strategies from the Sweet Science*
Advanced boxing skills and ring general-
ship.
978-1-884654-29-9 / $12.95
900 photos

No Holds Barred Fighting:
Takedowns
Throws, Trips, Drops and Slams for NHB
Competition and Street Defense
978-1-884654-25-1 / $12.95
850 photos

No Holds Barred Fighting:
The Clinch
Offensive and Defensive Concepts
Inside NHB's Most Grueling Position
978-1-884654-27-5 / $12.95
750 photos

No Holds Barred Fighting:
The Ultimate Guide to Conditioning
Elite Exercises and Training for NHB
Competition and Total Fitness
978-1-884654-29-9 / $12.95
900 photos

No Holds Barred Fighting:
The Kicking Bible
Strikes for MMA and the Street
978-1-884654-31-2 / $12.95
700 photos

No Second Chance:
A Reality-Based Guide to Self-Defense
How to avoid and survive an assault.
978-1-884654-32-9 / $12.95
500 photos

**No Holds Barred Fighting:
The Book of Essential Submissions**
How MMA champions gain their victo-
ries. A catalog of winning submissions.
978-1-884654-33-6 / $12.95
750 photos

**MMA Mastery: Flow Chain Drilling
and Integrated O/D Training
to Submission Wrestling**
Blends all aspects of the MMA fight
game into devastating performances.
978-1-884654-38-1 / $13.95
800 photos

MMA Mastery: Ground and Pound
A comprehensive go-to guide — how to
win on the ground.
978-1-884654-39-8 / $13.95
650 photos

MMA Mastery: Strike Combinations
Learn the savage efficiency of striking in
combinations. A comprehensive guide.
978-1-935937-22-7 / $12.95
1,000 photos

**Boxer's Book of
Conditioning & Drilling**
How to get fighting fit like the champions.
978-1-935937-28-9 / $12.95
650 photos

Boxer's Bible of Counterpunching
The Killer Response to Any Attack
978-1-935937-47-0 / $12.95
500 photos

Mud, Guts & Glory
Tips & Training for
Extreme Obstacle Racing
978-1-935937-56-2 / $12.95
500 photos

She's Tough
Extreme Fitness Training for Women
Kylie Hatmaker & Mark Hatmaker
978-1-935937-61-6 / $12.95
350 photos

Mark Hatmaker is the bestselling author of the *No Holds Barred Fighting Series,* the *MMA Mastery Series, No Second Chance* and *Boxing Mastery.* He also has produced more than 40 instructional

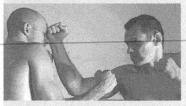

videos. His resume includes extensive experience in the combat arts including boxing, wrestling, Jiu-jitsu and Muay Thai.

He is a highly regarded coach of professional and amateur fighters, law enforcement officials and security personnel. Hatmaker founded Extreme Self Protection (ESP), a research body that compiles, analyzes and teaches the most effective Western combat methods known. ESP holds numerous seminars throughout the country each year including the prestigious Karate College/Martial Arts Universities in Radford, Virginia. He lives in Knoxville, Tennessee.

www.extremeselfprotection.com

TRACKS

Our sport instructional guides are bestsellers because each book contains hundreds of images, is packed with expert advice and retails at a great price. No one else comes close.

trackspublishing.com